SEASONS JOURNAL

SEASONS JOURNAL

ANALYZE THE SEASONS OF YOUR LIFE.
IMPACT GENERATIONS.

COMPANION TO *The Anchor*

Copyright @ 2020 by Mike Harvey.
All rights reserved.
ISBN: 978-0-578-75734-6

Unless approved, names or events have been intentionally disguised, and any resemblance to individuals is unintentional.

All Scripture quotations, unless otherwise indicated, are taken from the Holy Bible, New International Version®, NIV®. Copyright ©1973, 1978, 1984, 2011 by Biblica, Inc.™ Used by permission of Zondervan. All rights reserved worldwide. www.zondervan.com. The "NIV" and "New International Version" are trademarks registered in the United States Patent and Trademark Office by Biblica, Inc.™

Scriptures marked ESV are taken from the the Holy Bible, English Standard Version (ESV): Scriptures taken from the Holy Bible, English Standard Version®. Copyright© 2001 by Crossway, a publishing ministry of Good News Publishers. Used by permission.

Scriptures marked NKJV are taken from the New King James Version (NKJV): Scripture taken from the New King James Version®. Copyright© 1982 by Thomas Nelson, Inc. Used by permission. All rights reserved.

Scriptures marked NLT are taken from the Holy Bible, New Living Translation (NLT): Scriptures taken from the Holy Bible, New Living Translation, Copyright© 1996, 2004, 2007 by Tyndale House Foundation. Used by permission of Tyndale House Publishers, Inc., Carol Stream, Illinois 60188. All rights reserved. Used by permission.

impactothers.blog

PURPOSE:

Inspire others to reflect and write about their unique journey, impacting family, friends, and future generations.

It happened at 5:00 AM on a random morning. My dad's life suddenly ended and with it a lost opportunity to record his life for future generations. I never took the time to interview him or record his life story. I vowed that my kids would have my story.

So, I originally wrote The Anchor for my kids. I want to inspire them, have them learn from my mistakes, give them life lessons, and, ultimately, give them the gift of their dad's story.

Years later, I decided to inspire others to do the same. I know few will embark in writing a book, but, my hope is that the format of thinking through your life in seasons will give you an outline, at a minimum, to record your thoughts in a journal to inspire others.

Many parts of your story may be too painful to write. I found that out as I wrote about my journey. Additionally, some may never feel comfortable sharing parts of their story with their kids, much less generations. I understand that as well. In fact, I originally had two versions of the book, a "family" version for my kids and a version for my wife. Whatever you choose to include, I do hope that you give the gift of your journey to your family and others.

You have a story to tell. And, others, most importantly your family, will benefit immensely.

Contents

11   Define your Seasons

37   Season 1

57   Season 2

79   Season 3

101 Season 4

125 Season 5

145 Season 6

161 Season 7

177 Reflection

188 Lessons from your Journey

Potential Uses for the Seasons Journal

1. Personally, build your life story for friends, family, and future generations using the seasons format.
   - Maybe there are areas of your life that do not need to be revisited or discussed. Remember grace and skip the questions.
   - If you are at a middle life stage, record your seasons as you go. Additionally, focus on your threads and thinking through how you can control the weave of your personal tapestry.
   - If you are at an early life stage, spend your time thinking through seasons to date and your personal threads already developed.
2. Interview a loved one using the Seasons Journal, recording their life story for friends, family, and future generations.
   - A loved one may not have the health to work through the journal. Take action and make it happen. Your family will thank you.
3. Utilize the Seasons Journal as a marriage exercise, walking through a detailed sequence of events in your life with your spouse.
   - Each person should work each section independently, then discuss with their spouse.
4. Utilize the Seasons Journal as a small group exercise walking through your life with a small number of people.
   - The journal will work great to build a tight knit community, developing transparency, and learning that we are all on a unique journey with others.

If you decide to use this journal as a small group exercise, lead with grace. Stories are personal and may not want or need to be shared. Respect that.

Following is a suggestion for the study. Do your own thing, though. Go at your own pace.

Gathering 1: Read the preface and introduction of The Anchor. Work the "Seasons" section of the journal. Discuss The Anchor and the journal as a group.

Gathering 2: Read Season 1 of The Anchor and answer the questions for Season 1 in the journal. Discuss areas of The Anchor that can be applied to your own life and discuss the journal as a group.

Gathering 3: Read Season 2 of The Anchor and answer the questions for Season 2 in the journal. Discuss areas of The Anchor that can be applied to your own life and discuss the journal as a group.

Gathering 4: Read Season 3 of The Anchor and answer the questions for Season 3 in the journal. Discuss areas of The Anchor that can be applied to your own life and discuss the journal as a group.

Gathering 5: Read Season 4 of The Anchor and answer the questions for Season 4 in the journal. Discuss areas of The Anchor that can be applied to your own life and discuss the journal as a group.

Gathering 6: Read Season 5 of The Anchor and answer the questions for Season 5 thru 7 (if needed) in the journal. Discuss areas of The Anchor that can be applied to your own life and discuss the journal as a group.

Gathering 7: Read Reflection and 9 Lessons from The Anchor and complete the Reflection and Lessons section in the journal. Discuss each person's reflection and lessons as a group

Define your Seasons

Seasons of Life

As surely as the tide changes with the seasons and their weather, life changes. We change. We go through times of high tide and low, seasons that are calm and those that are tumultuous. Each season gradually dissipates into a fresh, new beginning. Before you know it, the years have flown by and there you stand looking back at your journey. That is why David Byrne's lyrics echo in my mind as I think about seasons: "How did I get here?" (For that reason, and because my friends and I used to imitate Byrne convulsing on stage in his live performance of the song.)

I believe it is a great thing to analyze your seasons. They help you know where you have been and, if you look closely, where you are going. After all, Solomon, the wise king of Israel, said there is nothing new under the sun (Ecc. 1:9). He also called life "meaningless" (12:8). Reflecting on his life, Solomon spoke of times in his life when he chased things in the world, saying these times were like chasing the wind (1:14).

If you look at the seasons of your life, you too will see that you were chasing things at different times, some meaningless, some meaningful. The meaningless times show the power of culture, the danger of folly, the inevitable picture of the fall of humanity. Oh, but the meaningful times. The times that are more than words can describe. The times that move the soul, like when you meet your wife or see your child for the first time. The meaningful times become etched in your mind, helping you remember the details of the season.

My story has all types of seasons—meaningful, meaningless, times that bring a tear to my eye or a smile to my face, times that make me fear, and times that make me want to convulse like David Byrne at the thought of the moment. The following is a sketch of my seasons that I wrote in April of 2018, reflecting on my life.

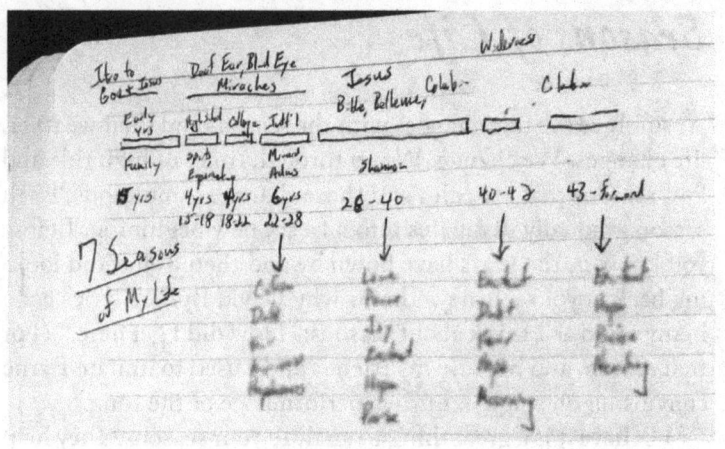

Purposely illegible, the drawing breaks my life down into seven different seasons, which I combined into five for The Anchor. After many twists and turns as I followed my unique path, I discovered how I was built, why I think like I do, and how to find an anchor in rough water.

My desire for The Anchor is that it would move you to likewise reflect on your own life. Don't waste the journey by floating through life without reflection. God sent you down your individual road for a reason. Find out what that is.

Seasons

Goal: Develop the seasonal outline of your life, considering 5 to 7 breaking points in your life, naming each season.

For illustrative purposes, my seasonal breaks follow.

Season 1 – The Foundation
Time period: birth to 15.
Broad Season Description: Early years, learning to do life.
Personal Characteristics: Innocence, simple, carefree.

Season 2 – Deaf Ear, Blind Eye, and Miracles
Time period: college to start of career.
Broad Season Description: New life, new friends, world travel.
Personal Characteristics: Fun, living for the moment, doubt, fear, anxiousness, hopelessness.

Season 3 – Grace
Time period: Mid-point in life.
Broad Season Description: Career change, marriage, kids
Personal Characteristics: Love, joy, peace, excitement, hope, praise.

Season 4 – Wilderness
Time period: Mid-point in life
Broad Season Description: Ministry, job change.
Personal Characteristics: Excitement, doubt, fear, hope, mourning.

Season 5 – Renewal
Time period: Mid-point in life
Broad Season Description: New song, new beginnings.
Personal Characteristics: Excitement, hope, praise.

Thought Starters to Develop your Seasons

This is the most critical piece of your story. Reflect and take your time. This section involves quite a bit of brainstorming, so you may want to use scratch paper before recording in your journal. Remember, this journal will be a gift to others, so you want the writing to be organized and legible.

When you think about different seasons in your life, I encourage you to think about mindset shifts, in addition to concrete life changes. For example, when I recognized the grace of God, I entered a different season. I viewed the world and people differently. On the flip side, one of my defined seasons changed when I entered college. Any seasonal break works. It is, after all, your story.

Each of the questions / statements below is designed to help you detail your seasons. Your seasons will more than likely be a combination of your answers to the questions below.

Name the 5+ most impactful events that happened in your life and write down the impact that each had on your life. Write down your age when each happened.

Thought starters: family moved cross country, college, day you met your spouse, child's birth, family sickness, 9/11, first job

_____

_____

_____

_____

_____

_____

_____

_____

_____

_____

_____

_____

_____

_____

_____

_____

_____

_____

Who were the 5+ people that had the biggest impact on your life? Describe why they had such as impact. Oftentimes, people coincide with seasonal changes. They help you see the world differently. Consider writing them a hand-written letter.

What were the 5+ biggest decisions you made in your life, and how did these choices change the course of your life? These may end up being great breaking points for each season.

Thought starters: college choice, decision to marry your spouse, decision to follow Jesus

Name the cities where you lived. What was your house like? What was the culture like?

Write down some of the ways you appear polished. What did you learn about jobs in the world your body could perform influence

Write down and describe every occupation you had. What did you learn at each job? How did your boss / coworkers influence you?

Stop and reflect on everything you have written. Your seasons should begin to come into view. I recommend 5 to 7 seasons. Now, use this page to sketch out your seasons.

Example, My Seasons

Season 1 – birth to 15

Breaking point to move to season 2 – loss of innocence, first drink of alcohol.

Season 2 – College to first job

Breaking point to move to season 3 – change of job, moved cities

Season 3 – Change in careers to Colombia

Breaking point to move to season 4 – Felt God moving me to do work in Colombia full time.

Season 4 – Work in Colombia

Breaking point to move to season 5 – Acceptance of job to move to a new city.

Season 5 – New city, job

Write your Seasons

Season 1–

Breaking point to move to season 2 –
_____
_____

Season 2 –

Breaking point to move to season 3 –
_____
_____

Season 3 –

Breaking point to move to season 4 –
_____
_____

Season 4 –

Breaking point to move to season 5 –
_____
_____

Season 5 –

Breaking point to move to season 6
_____
_____

Season 6 –

Breaking point to move to season 7 –

_____

_____

Season 7 –

_____

_____

Continue process if needed.

With this outline, add some detail to your seasons, using the following format.

Name the Season (i.e. The Early Years)

Detail the time period (i.e. birth to high school)

Give a broad season description (i.e. learned about life)

Write down personal characteristics (i.e. joy, hope-filled)

My Seasons

Season 1 – _____

Time period: _____

Broad Season Description:
_____
_____

Personal Characteristics:
_____
_____

Season 2 – _____

Time period: _____

Broad Season Description:
_____
_____

Personal Characteristics:
_____
_____

Season 3 – _____

Time period: _____

Broad Season Description:
_____
_____

Personal Characteristics:
_____

Season 4 – _____

Time period: _____

Broad Season Description:
_____
_____

Personal Characteristics:
_____
_____

Season 5 – _____

Time period: _____

Broad Season Description:
_____
_____

Personal Characteristics:
_____
_____

Season 6 – _____

Time period: _____

Broad Season Description:
_____
_____

Personal Characteristics:
_____
_____

Season 7 – _____

Time period: _____

Broad Season Description: _____
_____
_____

Personal Characteristics: _____
_____
_____

Think through each Season

Now that you have your life broken down into seasons, this journal will lead you through a series of questions pertaining to each individual season. Remember, the journal will be a gift to your family and friends. Spend time in deep thinking to make sure you record what you want them to know.

For each section, I have included a write-up of my season from The Anchor. My hope is that my write-up will help you began to start thinking about your own season.

You'll see that an important piece of your season, invaluable to your family and future generations, is the identification and recording of your personal threads. I define a "thread" as a certain characteristic or trait that makes you who you are. For example, my dad was an independent worker, not prone to following rules. Rules were guidelines in his life. He wanted to do things his way, extremely efficiently. As I thought about my life, I discovered that I have this exact thread in my own life, almost mimicking my dad. I now know this thread is woven into my tapestry, and I manage it effectively.

Discovering your threads is an invaluable tool to help you discover who you are, how you were built.

Season 1

Season 1 – The Foundation

And the rain fell, and the floods came, and the winds blew and beat on that house, but it did not fall, because it had been founded on the rock.

—Matthew 7:25 (ESV)

Formative, family, fun. These are the words that describe my early years. I was blessed to grow up with an incredible family in a great community. Though I didn't always, I now know looking back the value of that.

My family was fun, safe, and secure. We had tight relationships, and I so enjoyed our time together. My dad was the leader, respected, feared, and loved. My mom loved my dad and always had my back. Divorce was never even a thought, and you didn't hear about it much in life. In fact, I can't think of one instance of divorce in our neighborhood.

With two brothers and a sister, competitiveness was instilled in me at a young age. There was always some type of game going on, whether it be inside hoops, outside hoops, or Wiffle Ball. I had to learn quickly how to control my emotions in the heat of the moment and how to win or else handle the trash talk.

There were things I could depend on, like family dinners. There were always six people around the table, and Mom always had casseroles, fresh vegetables, and sweet tea.

We routinely took family vacations, driving cross country like the Griswolds. At that time, in my community, there was no flying in airplanes. All the families drove. Summer always found us headed somewhere new and exciting, like Washington, D.C. or the beach or the mountains.

As most kids, I assumed everyone's life was similar to mine. At the time, in the '70s and '80s, the world was still a big place. The intricate details of the world were not known broadly. Computers, social media, and cell phones didn't exist. I couldn't look on my device at Bali, Indonesia to see the beautiful beaches. I didn't understand the poverty that existed in the Amazon jungle.

Outside of missing the next neighborhood Wiffle Ball game, I didn't have fears. War and hate weren't a part of my life. I didn't even know what prejudice or terrorism were at the time. A common fear among kids today is the fear of someone entering a movie theater with a gun and opening fire. That would have been a crazy thought to me. The world I knew was a safe place.

Comparisons weren't a part of my world either. As a kid, I don't remember labeling people as rich or poor or by what kind of house they lived in or by the car they drove or by the school they attended. None of this mattered. I was not in the middle of a "keep up with the Joneses" environment.

By today's standards, my neighborhood was abnormal. However, I suppose back then it was normal. The community was full of kids with the freedom to come and go as they pleased. We kids learned life together, formed a bond, a band of brothers and sisters.

The thought of life in rural Mississippi brings back special memories. I am who I am today because of it. The threads woven into my fabric during this season in large part composed the life that I live today.

We are all given threads in life, certain characteristics and traits that make us who we are. Some threads we are born with, and some we acquire along the way. This is not a process we control; we do not select the threads we are handed. We can, however, control the weaving. We must. We cannot sit by idly and allow the world to make of us whatever it chooses.

Throughout my early years, I had to cut some of the threads being woven into my life so that they would not be the predominant colors of my fabric. Others, however, I embraced, allowing them to be more defining.

Done well, our threads can be a lifeline, a guide. Our threads can help us manage the journey through life. The uncontrollables are inevitable, but the threads that display who we are can provide a point of reference, a perspective from which to view the world, a deep understanding of who we are and where we are going.

Threads in the Foundational Season

Looking back, I realize the threads, both given and acquired, in the early years of my life made me who I am as a person today. As I mentioned at the beginning of the chapter, the threads can be positive and negative. The key is controlling the weave.

My fabric contained the beneficial threads of religion, work ethic, the "get it done" mentality, and a positive view of family. Some of my negative threads included alcoholism, the desire to be perceived as strong, and the ability to wear a façade and keep skeletons locked in a closet.

As you continue reading my journey, you will begin to see the impact of my foundational threads. The traits have always been there, through no choice of my own, but I would allow both the positive and negative traits to manifest themselves at different times. I would do little to control the weave.

Even today, my daily battle is to control my negative threads, because these will never go away. They are part of my tapestry, yes. However, I must stop them from surfacing so that their colors do not define who I am.

The positive threads given to me in adolescence, on the other hand, are my engine, propelling me in this world. I thank God for my foundational threads.

Season 1 - _____

Time Period in Life:

_____
_____
_____

Describe your early home life, your parents, your earliest remembrance of life.
Note: For some, this reflection could be extremely painful, with no desire to revisit. If so, maybe just outline a few thoughts, such as the city where you lived or your church.

_____
_____
_____
_____
_____
_____
_____
_____
_____
_____
_____
_____
_____
_____
_____
_____
_____

Name the 5+ most impactful events that happened in your life and write down the impact that each had on your life. Some of the events may be repeated from the broad seasons exercise, but other events will come into focus when you dial into this particular season.

Who are the 5 people that had the biggest positive impact on your life during this season? You answered this question broadly about your life as you developed your seasons. Now, dial into this particular season.

What would you say to each person if you could? Consider writing them each a letter. The note would mean the world to them.

What core beliefs were developed?

_____
_____
_____
_____
_____
_____
_____
_____

View of people (stereotypes, ethnicity). Why did you have this belief?

_____
_____
_____
_____
_____
_____
_____
_____
_____

View of the world (big/small, fears, travel). Why did you have this belief?

_____
_____
_____

View of religion or church. Why did you have this belief?

View of God. Why did you have this belief?

What impact did the area where you grew up have on your life? (city, state, area country)

What storms came into your life during this season and what was the impact of these storms?

What threads were developed during this season and why? Thought starters – independent thinking, work ethic, view of religion, alcoholism

What are the evidences of God's grace from this season?

Looking over this season, what are 3+ pieces of advice you give your family, friends, the world.

Additional thoughts that I want captured for my family and friends about Season 1.

Season 2

Season 2 – Deaf Ear, Blind Eye, and Miracles

> *For this people's heart has grown dull,*
> *and with their ears they can barely hear,*
> *and their eyes they have closed,*
> *lest they should see with their eyes*
> *and hear with their ears*
> *and understand with their heart*
> *and turn, and I would heal them.*
>
> —*Matthew 13:15 (ESV)*

I watched the young man mowing our back yard with a tear in my eye. A week earlier he had lost his dad, only fifty-one years old. His dad was a great man who cared for the lawns of half the people in my neighborhood. He worked with excellence. The neighborhood had a love and respect for him. A week earlier, I had talked to him about making sure our gate was closed after he finished cutting the grass. Now, I was talking to his son, telling him that I was sorry and praying for him and his family. An abrupt, unexpected end to his dad's life, and an unplanned twist in his.

The journey always has unexpected twists and turns. Any security we look for in this world cannot be found. Health, money, and the best of relationships will all let you down when you least expect it. Look around, examine humanity and you will see that this is an absolute truth. We live in an unstable world. That is why we need an anchor.

We lull ourselves into thinking we have complete control of life. We create a bubble, a seemingly indestructible defense against the potential storms in life. But the inevitable storm will come.

Reflecting on my foundational years, I realize the blessed life that I lived during that early season. However, in the moment, rarely do you take time to reflect on your seasons, your journey. This is especially true in your youth. I was oblivious to the blessings I had received early in life. I thought everyone was like me.

So, I entered season two eager to do life my way, chart my own course. Maybe it was because I was the youngest of four, or maybe it was because of the competitive nature instilled in me at a young age, but whatever the case, I was only concerned about the here and now and what I wanted to do in the moment. My mindset was not set on the long-term, where I wanted to go, what I wanted to be. I was never imagining what the future would be like. I was young and on top of the world. Implied in this thinking was that I was in complete control.

Sure, I believed in God, at least I thought I did, but my belief had never been challenged. After all, I lived in a bubble in Mississippi, oblivious to the outside world. This bubble created a misconception of control, a life in which dependence on God was not valued or needed.

Consequently, I shelved God and focused on myself. I entered this season focused on the things of this world, concerned about friends, sports, and being a social leader. Without my recognizing it, my life was molded into the culture of the time. Whatever was popular, whatever was fun, whatever made me edgy and gave me the appearance of fearlessness, I was in. There were few barriers, other than trying to fly under the radar of any authority, such as my parents.

On top of all the threads already woven into my fabric were added the threads of independence and leadership, both good qualities if controlled. I wanted independence, to do things my way. This fierce independence naturally created leadership. If my friends were afraid, I would go first as a leader. I become somewhat of a compass for those close to me.

The overarching thought was that I would live forever. The Bible describes this as the folly of youth (Prov. 22:15). As I reflect, in some instances, I wonder who this person was. If you only knew me in this season, you would be baffled at who I am today. That is the beauty of seasons. Just like a lifeless, dormant plant in the winter comes to a vibrant work of art in the spring, such is a life with the ebb and flow of seasons.

But, all of that deep thinking can wait. During this season, it was time to take on the world with no filters. Like a sailboat without a sail, left to be blown wherever the wind led, I was ready to follow life anywhere. I had no anchor, and I didn't feel I needed an anchor. Ironically, I loved the Talking Heads song, "Road to Nowhere."

Threads of the Season of Deaf Ears, Blind Eyes, and Miracles

During this season, from college to the start of my career, new threads took root. Most of these threads were gifts of experience from the opportunities I had. My eyes were opened to people with different worldviews, different cultures, and different ways of doing life.

With all of this change, I learned to mold to fit any environment. I became a chameleon that could perform in social settings or business settings. I developed a thread of keeping things behind closed doors, under wraps. I never wanted to be perceived as being fearful of anything, any person or situation. Reminds me of my dad.

I began to push limits further and further, giving me a thread of risk-taking too. I wanted to be the leader and accordingly pushed whomever I was with to new experiences, new highs, new places. Danger was masked by intensity.

Additionally, many of my threads from early in life began to materialize in this season of discovery. For example, as I mentioned, the thread of working hard was given to me by my dad and the way he did life. Well, this thread manifested itself when I received my first job in college. I didn't count the hours that I was on the clock, as I could outwork anyone. Today's mindset of "work–life balance" didn't exist for me. I just worked hard, playing the one string that I knew I could play.

The thread of alcohol began to show up in the form of binge drinking. This thread led me to narcotics. Negative threads must be controlled, suppressed, but I did not attempt to mask this color at all. Threads were given complete freedom to go wherever they wanted. There was no direction, no vision, no strategy. And as a result, the tapestry of my life became a mess.

When people looked at me, there was little to find of benefit. My example only led them further down a destructive path. Yes, I wanted to lead and did so swiftly and proudly, but I didn't recognize the implications of the influence my threads were having on other people. If I could have understood and controlled these tendencies earlier in life, what a positive impact I could have made.

But, that is the thing about life and your individual tapestry. Although your tapestry is a picture of you, the threads bleed over into other lives. You must handle with care or face regret, which is never what you want in life.

Season 2 - _____

Time Period in Life:

_____
_____

What are the 3 to 5 decisions that most impacted your life during this season and describe how the decisions changed your life.

Who are the 5 people that had the biggest positive impact on your life, and what would you say to each person if you could? Consider writing them each a letter. The note would mean the world to them.

How did the season 1 impact season 2?

_____
_____
_____
_____
_____
_____
_____
_____

How did your beliefs on religion and God play out in season 2?

_____
_____
_____
_____
_____
_____
_____
_____

How did your view of people from season 1 impact you in season 2?

_____
_____
_____

_____
_____
_____
_____
_____

Did the area where you grew up impact your journey in season 2?

_____
_____
_____
_____
_____
_____
_____
_____
_____
_____
_____
_____

What storms came into your life during this season and what was the impact of these storms?

What threads were developed during this season and why?

What are the evidences of God's grace from this season?

What was your anchor during this season?

Looking over this season, what are 3+ pieces of advice you give your family, friends, the world.

Additional thoughts that I want captured for my family and friends about Season 2.

Season 3

Season 3 – Grace

For by grace you have been saved through faith. And this is not your own doing; it is the gift of God, 9 not a result of works, so that no one may boast.

—*Ephesians 2:8-9 (ESV)*

For ten years, my journey had been one of new experiences, new cultures, new views of the world. From college to my work abroad, I had seen the good, the bad, and the ugly. And the amazing part: I was still alive.

As far as success is defined in our culture, I guess I had achieved it. I now had experience that would allow my career to blossom in any of several different directions, and I was with a company that had endless growth opportunities. I was in a great position.

But, for some reason, I felt like I was missing out. My friends looked at my life and were impressed with my travels, my success. Not one of them could match my experiences since college. Many were making more money, but no one had the worldview that I now had. Whenever I was back in the States, attending weddings or parties, my college friends and their new friends would pepper me with questions about my travels. I was on a pedestal.

I, however, was blind to the value of my experiences. In my mind, I was simply behind. As I looked around at my peers and saw blossoming marriages, kids, houses, and seemingly stable lives, I felt like I had wasted the last handful of years traveling internationally. I had always pictured myself married with a house and kids, but I was nowhere near that. I felt like I was a nomad rambling the earth. Every time I was around my old crew, I felt that I didn't belong.

Reflecting now, it's amazing to me that I did not recognize the incredible journey I'd been on. That season of my life was a gift, a blessing. It provided me great wisdom, opened my eyes to possibilities, and developed a foundation that allowed me to embrace the world with no fear. At the time, though, I only saw what I thought I was missing. I was blinded by culture.

Culture will eat your lunch if you let it. Culture beckons you to file in, to do life a certain way, by a certain age. Culture fools you into to thinking that there are certain parameters for success. Instead of playing my game, enjoying the journey God had created for me, I wanted to imitate other people and their journeys. I had been given this unique path, but I wanted to be like others.

Longing for something different, I decided the fast life that I had been living had to slow down, whatever that meant. I felt like I needed to move closer to home, reengage with my old friends, and change my course to one that was more familiar. In other words, I needed to mold my life to look like the lives of my friends.

I entered the next season with my eyes set on finding a stable bubble, much like the Mississippi bubble I had emerged from. I wanted a safe little comfortable life. Those aren't the terms I would have used back then to describe my goals, but that summarizes my mindset. And the first step: I needed to move closer to my family and, more importantly, my old college friends.

For some reason, I never recognized any danger in reengaging with my old friends. I thought that after ten years I would magically appear back in Memphis and life would be the same as it was in college. However, everyone you meet is in a unique season of life too. I would soon discover that not one of my friends had a "safe little comfortable life." Like me, everyone else was also feeling tossed about by the waves, trying to make sense of the course they were on, and all were without an anchor.

The fallacy of life is that one can somehow "arrive." We all long for it, run after it, the feeling of success, victory, and unending peace. We mark dates on calendars and say things like, "If I can just make it to this point, things will be great."

Unfortunately, or fortunately, this date never arrives. In every case, success, victory, and unending peace will finally be recognized as a mirage. Only then, when you realize that the world has nothing to offer, will you be enlightened. There you will discover peace. And the interesting thing about this discovery is that, if embraced, you will find yourself on the most daring adventure that you have ever been on in your life. The world will suddenly have meaning. Don't shrink back from the adventure. An anchor is available for the journey.

Threads of the Season of Grace

I entered this third season feeling behind in life, a little on edge as I looked around at the lives of my friends. I left this season a new person with a new life and a new purpose. The season of grace forever changed my life.

The thread of perspective was a welcome addition to my tapestry. I had a new perspective on others, their journeys, their lives. I faced the deaths of friends, which helped me understand the brevity of life. And I gained a better perspective of God, how big he is. Perspective ultimately helped me be brave, fear nothing, and have active faith. This is one thread, however, that I must continually magnify to receive its full benefit.

My entrepreneurial spirit was birthed in this season. I developed a love for small business and creating things. I believe I always had the spark in me from my upbringing, but the fire was lit during this season.

Love became a thread at this time too. Not love like we tend to say in our culture when we really mean that we like things, but love as in "two become one." With this thread, selfishness is relinquished and you live for someone else. This thread gives life, new meaning to why you are here.

Perhaps the most powerful thread to be woven into my fabric during this season, though, was the thread of absolute truth. Absolute truth is gained from the Bible, so essentially, I became biblically literate during this season. I now know what the book says.

Although culture would say this thread is abrasive, it is anything but that. Absolute truth, which comes from the Bible, says that we are all the same, full of sin. At our core, we are all messed-up people trying to find our way. None is better than the other. The thread of absolute truth gave me a new worldview, a lens through which to view everything, and it became my anchor in rough seas.

All of these thoughts and threads woven together made me risk-averse. But I came to feel that the safe, comfortable bubble that I had created was not my destiny. God wanted more from me, the opposite of safety.

Interesting. I began this season looking for what I described as a safe, comfortable bubble. I ended the season wanting to bust the bubble and live a life going after God, anything but safe.

Season 3 - _____

Time Period in Life:
_____
_____
_____

What are the 3 to 5 decisions that most impacted your life during this season and describe how the decisions changed your life.

_____
_____
_____
_____
_____
_____
_____
_____
_____
_____
_____
_____
_____
_____
_____
_____
_____
_____
_____

Who are the 5 people that had the biggest positive impact on your life, and what would you say to each person if you could? Consider writing them each a letter. The note would mean the world to them.

How did the season 2 impact season 3?

How did your beliefs on religion and God play out in season 3?

How did your view of people from season 1 impact you in season 3?

Did the area where you grew up impact your journey in season 3?

What storms came into your life during this season and what was the impact of these storms?

What threads were developed during this season and why?

What are the evidences of God's grace from this season?

What was your anchor during this season?

Looking over this season, what are 3+ pieces of advice you give your family, friends, the world.

Additional thoughts that I want captured for my family and friends about Season 3.

Season 4

Season 4 – The Wilderness

And behold, I am with you always, to the end of the age.

—MATTHEW 28:20 (ESV)

The wilderness. A lonely place full of fear, with no direction to safety. A place where all hope vanishes. Nothing make senses. You look for stability, a safety net, an anchor, but the world offers no peace. The wilderness causes panic, anxiety, and overwhelming thoughts. And, the wilderness comes swiftly.

You will not see the wilderness coming. If you did, you would change course. After all, we spend our lives doing everything to avoid the wilderness, don't we? We try to live the American dream—a nice, safe life free from danger and risk and surrounded by the comforts of our culture.

Consequently, our kids are raised in bubbles, an unfair picture of things to come. They grow and end up following culture, filing in, staying on the path. We inadvertently teach that the game of life is a game of striving for comfort and materialism. We inadvertently teach that life isn't about Jesus but about safety.

Because of our desire for comfort, we mold our beliefs into a different brand of Christianity. We create a different Jesus. A Jesus who desires our comfort in this world.

With this mindset, we are not mentally or spiritually prepared for the difficult times. The wilderness blindsides us, and we are shaken to the core. Only then do we look for an anchor. Only then do we tend to run to our Father.

A great example of this for me is what happened on 9/11. Our world was rocked. My world was rocked. When I showed up at church the following Sunday, we had to walk a mile to get in the building. Everyone was at church. At the most desperate point in their lives, in the wilderness, people sprinted to the church, as they were looking for solid ground.

Now, I am not saying we should not be running here. We should. We must run to Jesus when in the wilderness. I am, however, saying that we must not wait until the wilderness to run to the cross, as if Jesus is some type of genie to be called upon when we need wishes granted to get us out of hard times. We must prepare for the seasons of want now.

An absolute truth in this world is that you will find yourself in the wilderness. Wilderness will come to everyone. It may take the form of money. You may lose it all. Or maybe it will manifest as sickness or death, in which case money means nothing. Wilderness might even be mental battles of stress, depression, or loneliness. No one can say what wilderness you will face, but it will happen, so I encourage you to prepare.

The best way I know to prepare for the wilderness is to pick up your Bible. Become biblically literate. Understand who God really is, not who culture says he is. Don't shy away from the light that is found in God's Word, for this is the only light that will guide you in the darkness of the wilderness.

Thankfully, I knew God and his Word intimately when I stepped into the wilderness. To say I was fully prepared, though, would be a lie. At forty, my life was seemingly great. My family, my business, and my ministry were all blessed beyond belief. Everything I touched seemed to succeed. I think that I was fooled into thinking that there was no wilderness, not for me at least. I didn't realize I was headed there.

As you'll see, the wilderness came suddenly. I found myself looking around, second-guessing everything in my life. I had never been in a situation of having to lead my family when I did not know the path we would take. My wife and I were looking at an unknown future. Her faith was unwavering, but I must admit, I questioned mine. I heard Dr. Rogers say one time, "If you have never doubted your faith, then I doubt you are a Christian." Well, I can now check that box.

Even still, though, in the middle of it all, I knew that I was doubting something that was absolutely true. In fact, I would constantly tell myself that I did not want to look back at this period in my life and remember that I'd turned from my faith. I wanted to look at the wilderness and remember how I clung to God.

And I did cling to God. I had trouble praying, believing, and having faith, but I clung to my Father. Often this just looked like inwardly reciting what I knew Jesus said in Matthew 28:20: "I am with you always, to the very end of the age." Biblical literacy. I can't stress it enough. It was so important for me during the wilderness season when I had little else to work with. I thank God that he prepared me and gave me an anchor.

Threads from the Wilderness Season

As I reflect on the last chapter of our life in Memphis, I realize that I have severely understated the challenge it presented to me as a husband, father, and leader of my family.

My personal battle was in an area that would have been unknown had it not been for the gift of the wilderness. Yes, the wilderness was a gift. Because the center of the struggle in the wilderness was where I found my self-worth. It would have remained dormant forever had God not interceded and led us through this season.

Prior to this time, I inadvertently tied my self-worth to professional equity and the wealth that I created. My career, my status, my money defined me. People knew me as a successful businessperson, and I craved this admiration. I depended on my career and my wealth for my happiness.

Wealth is the great blind spot, especially in the United States. Maybe that is why Jesus talked more about money than any other subject. The Bible doesn't say that money is the root of all evil but that the love of money is the root of all evil (1 Tim. 6:10). One may claim that Jesus is number one in their life, that they depend on him for all, that they have great faith, but I don't believe that you ever realize your dependence on wealth and your career until it is ripped away. After all, why do you need faith when you have all the material wealth that you will ever need?

If you don't think you are wealthy, it's possible you need to reevaluate. Compared to the majority of the world that lives on four dollars a day, most of us in the United States are ridiculously wealthy.

I have a spiritual mentor who lives in the Amazon jungle running an orphanage. She lives on about five hundred dollars a month, constantly going without to provide for the kids. This meek warrior in a small body tells many stories of how God showed up when all hope was lost. She is 100 percent dependent on her God to care for her and provide for her. He is enough. Her self-worth is found in her Lord. I have never seen dependence on God like from this mentor of mine. Her faith is extreme. It makes me uncomfortable and convicts me to my core. I want this faith.

So to me, the thread, the gift, given to me during the wilderness was new vision, the ability to see the indirect correlation between wealth and faith. As wealth increases, faith decreases. It has to, as you don't need anything. And as wealth decreases, faith increases. It has to, because you are forced to depend on God. I try to magnify this new vision thread in my tapestry.

For all those out there who are saying, "If I can just make a little more money" or "If I can just move into this position, then I will be content," beware. The price paid could be your faith. I know that this is hard to believe, because we are lulled into thinking pridefully that our faith is great, our dependence on God is great. That is exactly why the dependence on wealth is a blind spot.

A great test is what the traveling minister Manley Beasley would always say: what are you depending on right now that would leave you sunk if it went away? Most often, the answer is money. It was for me, until the wilderness removed the scales from my eyes.

Indeed, leaving my job to focus on the work in Colombia, from an earthly standpoint, was a horrible career and financial move. I thought I had counted the costs, but I had no idea. I lost a whole lot of money, and I lost a whole lot of professional equity. I essentially started over on both. Everything that I valued on earth from a professional standpoint was gone.

I question a lot, did I really recognize God's will for my life when I left my job for Colombia? Was this decision emotionally driven? Did I miss it? Here's the deal. Outside of the direct truths in God's Word, I am never 100 percent sure of his will. I can talk myself out of things. I can pray myself out of things. So, if I think that God is calling me to do something and I am over 50 percent confident that he is indeed calling, I will go. I have to go. That is faith. That is obedience. The outcome of the journey is in God's hands, and from reading Scripture, I know that it is never easy. In fact, it cost the people in the Bible a lot, and, it cost me a lot too. That is okay. I obey knowing that his ways are not my ways. I am thankful that God gave me faith to trust.

I also battle the thought of what my life would look like if I had not left my career. Honestly, I would be nearing an early retirement, as I had done a tremendous job of saving. Culture constantly presses into me with this thought.

For example, I was recently having dinner with a couple of God-fearing men. I recounted the story to them, and one of them said, in a sarcastic tone, "How did that decision work out for you?" Seriously, brother?

I still battle these thoughts and other falsehoods, and I must regularly give them to God. I imagine that I will battle these thoughts forever.

God is my rock, my Redeemer, my anchor. He is my hope. I depend on him. I believe that is why he put me on the journey that he did. He wanted me to depend on him more. I pray that I decrease and he increases (John 3:30).

I am thankful for a God who cares for his children like he does.

Season 4 - _____

Time Period in Life:
_____

What are the 3 to 5 decisions that most impacted your life during this season and describe how the decisions changed your life.
_____
_____
_____
_____
_____
_____
_____
_____
_____
_____
_____
_____
_____
_____
_____
_____
_____
_____

Who are the 5 people that had the biggest positive impact on your life, and what would you say to each person if you could? Consider writing them each a letter. The note would mean the world to them.

How did the season 3 impact season 4?

_____
_____
_____
_____
_____
_____
_____
_____

How did your beliefs on religion and God play out in season 4?

_____
_____
_____
_____
_____
_____
_____
_____

How did your view of people from season 1 impact you in season 4?

_____
_____
_____
_____

Did the area where you grew up impact your journey in season 4?

What storms came into your life during this season and what was the impact of these storms?

What threads were developed during this season and why?

What are the evidences of God's grace from this season?

What was your anchor during this season?

Looking over this season, what are 3+ pieces of advice you give your family, friends, the world.

Additional thoughts that I want captured for my family and friends about Season 4.

Additional thoughts that I wish to share for my own and the reader's sake.

Season 5

Season 5 – Renewal

*I had heard of you by the hearing of the ear,
but now my eye sees you;*

—Job 42:5 (ESV)

Renewal. On this stretch of the journey, the wilderness is quickly forgotten and optimism rules the day. Life is met with a feeling of invigoration and bullishness. A chance to start over.

The renewal season, indeed, is sweet. For me, this season of life was full of hope, excitement, and happiness. As the leader of my family, emerging from the wilderness, I had direction and strategy before me. This felt good.

As for my wife, she was being a faithful partner, obedient to her husband, but ultimately, Shannon just wanted to follow God. If he was leading, she wanted to file in.

Our kids were young and resilient. They were good with the move and would soon forget our lives in Memphis. Northwest Arkansas would be their home.

This is not to say, though, that the season of renewal is an easy one. Life would never be the same for my family. When I made the decision to leave my job in Memphis to focus on Colombia, ships were burned. We had to begin a new journey into uncharted waters.

The joy of leaving Memphis was that God had provided and we were following him. We would be leaving the wilderness to a place uniquely planned for us. Shannon and I knew this deep in our hearts, so our faith brought us comfort.

However, the pain was ever-present. We had lived in Memphis fifteen years around our church, our friends, our ministry, our business, our families, everything that we seemingly cared about. We loved Memphis, and our roots were deep in this city.

More than anything, though, the thought of leaving our friends hurt, and it especially hurt Shannon. As I've said, we had deep friendships that were like family relationships. There is a depth of relationship that develops between families when you go through different stages together, like marriage, the birth and growth of children, and the deepening of faith. A bond is formed that will never be taken away. This bond is to be cherished. It is a gift of God.

But, following God is greater than the things of this world. It must be. The world is not our home. Although Shannon and I had read this truth many times in the Bible, we were now being taught what it meant. God was refining us, and refining is never fun or easy, but it is good.

Threads from the Renewal Season

The word *renewal* means "to make like new...restore to freshness, vigor, or perfection."5 No doubt, this was a season of renewal. However, renewal for the Harvey's was anything but easy. The journey has been difficult but blessed.

The thing about renewal is that the season doesn't change who you are at your core or your past. Your old threads arrive with you and continue to weave as you navigate the twists and turns of the new season. The threads are permanent placements in your soul. The key to journeying well is how you manage them. Know them and steer them well.

There are also new threads that emerge during this season, though. For me, probably the biggest new thread is what I call maturity. The Bible speaks of spiritual maturity coming as one understands God more. I gained a deeper understanding of my Father. Things change, but he remains the same.

Spiritual maturity only comes from spending time with God, mainly in his Word. In spending time with him, one begins to understand more and more of his character. The more I walk with God, the more I understand, the more I love, the more I realize how I need him.

Left to my own thoughts and opinions, void of Scripture, I twist religion and the character of God into how I think it should be. I try to make sense of things through my view of the world. God is God, though. He created all. His ways are not my ways. This side of heaven, I will never completely understand his sovereignty. But, I understand more of his love for me after growing in spiritual maturity in my renewal season.

Another thread I picked up—or really, refined—was the thread of adaptability. After spending fifteen years in a place that is home, one must be incredibility adaptable to take on a new culture. Church is not the same, people are not the same, your life is not the same. During the renewal season, I learned not to fight the cultural difference but understand it, embrace it.

And then there is what is perhaps the sweetest part of a renewal season: the time it allows you to catch your breath and view your tapestry, your journey, with clarity. When the speed, confusion, and stress clear, you realize that God was walking with you the whole time. You turn around and see that the path you have been walking is illuminated. I suppose this is when you understand the value of the anchor. You see how God controlled the entire journey and how your threads have come together to form a magnificent picture.

Though the ship rocks at times in the rough sea, the anchor holds.

Season 5 - _____

Time Period in Life:
_____
_____
_____

What are the 3 to 5 decisions that most impacted your life during this season and describe how the decisions changed your life.

Who are the 5 people that had the biggest positive impact on your life, and what would you say to each person if you could? Consider writing them each a letter. The note would mean the world to them.

14. Who are those people that had the worst hospitality happen to you? How can you pray for them and bless them? Even consider writing them each a letter like we would write to an enemy combatant.

How did the season 4 impact season 5?
_____
_____
_____
_____
_____
_____
_____
_____

How did your beliefs on religion and God play out in season 5?
_____
_____
_____
_____
_____
_____
_____
_____

How did your view of people from season 1 impact you in season 5?
_____
_____
_____

Did the area where you grew up impact your journey in season 5?

What storms came into your life during this season and what was the impact of these storms?

What threads were developed during this season and why?

What are the evidences of God's grace from this season?

What was your anchor during this season?

Looking over this season, what are 3+ pieces of advice you give your family, friends, the world.

_____
_____
_____
_____
_____
_____
_____
_____
_____
_____
_____
_____
_____
_____
_____
_____
_____
_____
_____
_____
_____
_____
_____
_____
_____
_____
_____

Additional thoughts that I want captured for my family and friends about Season 5.

Season 6

Season 6 - _____

Time Period in Life:
_____
_____

What are the 3 to 5 decisions that most impacted your life during this season and describe how the decisions changed your life.

_____
_____
_____
_____
_____
_____
_____
_____
_____
_____
_____
_____
_____
_____
_____
_____
_____

Who are the 5 people that had the biggest positive impact on your life, and what would you say to each person if you could? Consider writing them each a letter. The note vwould mean the world to them.

How did the season 5 impact season 6?

_____
_____
_____
_____
_____
_____
_____
_____
_____

How did your beliefs on religion and God play out in season 6?

_____
_____
_____
_____
_____
_____
_____
_____
_____

How did your view of people from season 1 impact you in season 6?

_____
_____
_____
_____

Did the area where you grew up impact your journey in season 6?

What storms came into your life during this season and what was the impact of these storms?

What threads were developed during this season and why?

What are the evidences of God's grace from this season?

What was your anchor during this season?

Looking over this season, what are 3+ pieces of advice you give your family, friends, the world.

Additional thoughts that I want captured for my family and friends about Season 6.

Season 7

Season 7 - _____

Time Period in Life:
_____
_____

What are the 3 to 5 decisions that most impacted your life during this season and describe how the decisions changed your life.

_____
_____
_____
_____
_____
_____
_____
_____
_____
_____
_____
_____
_____
_____
_____
_____
_____
_____
_____

Who are the 5 people that had the biggest positive impact on your life, and what would you say to each person if you could? Consider writing them each a letter. The note would mean the world to them.

How did the season 6 impact season 7?

_____
_____
_____
_____
_____
_____
_____
_____

How did your beliefs on religion and God play out in season 7?

_____
_____
_____
_____
_____
_____
_____
_____

How did your view of people from season 1 impact you in season 7?

_____
_____
_____

Did the area where you grew up impact your journey in season 7?

What storms came into your life during this season and what was the impact of these storms?

What threads were developed during this season and why?

What are the evidences of God's grace from this season?

What was your anchor during this season?

Looking over this season, what are 3+ pieces of advice you give your family, friends, the world.

Additional thoughts that I want captured for my family and friends about Season 7.

Reflection

Reflection

> *But one thing I do: Forgetting what is behind and straining toward what is ahead*
>
> —PHILIPPIANS 3:13

As I walked into my new church this morning, I saw new faces. New people greeted me, and a new community awaited. None knew the threads woven into my fabric, my journey, or my life perspective, and I didn't know theirs. I only knew I was among individuals who each had threads, each had traveled a journey unknown to the outside world. I wondered what the world, this church, our class would look like if we took off the masks and let others see our tapestries.

One thing I know all of our tapestries would show: the only anchor in life that holds is God. And the way to understand and stay connected to the anchor is through his Word. Life offers no other stability.

As I finish the story about our lives up to this point, I am not sure what God has in store in the future for the Harvey's. I only know that God himself is with us, a promise he gave us in Matthew 28:20. There is great, unsurpassed peace in that verse. I couldn't live without it, as I know he has forgiven much.

The Bible tells the story of a man named Simon. Simon was a fisherman, the sea his hunting ground. One day, as he was pulling his net in on the beach by the Sea of Galilee, Jesus approached him, looking deep into his eyes. The Bible uses the Greek word *emblepo* to describe the gaze. *Emblepo* means to "look upon" with a "close, penetrating 'look.'"6 Jesus, being God himself, looked at Simon and knew all that would happen in his life. He knew that Simon would say that he was committed but turn his back on him at his darkest hour. He knew that Simon's passion and tendencies to speak his mind would get him in trouble throughout his life. And he knew that Simon would never, could never, live a life without failure.

Yet, even knowing all of these shortcomings, Jesus didn't

condemn or pass Simon by to find someone who could better measure up. Not Jesus. Not him who was grace himself. Instead, at that moment, looking in his eyes, Jesus changed Simon's name to Peter, meaning "rock." At that moment, Jesus said that Peter would be a rock for his ministry, the church. Jesus overlooked the failures of Simon and welcomed the man Peter with open arms, giving him a life of immeasurable purpose, joy, and hope. In a moment, Peter's life changed forever.

And so it is with me. Like Peter, my life is full of failures and shortcomings. However, when Jesus first gazed into my eyes, he knew that. He knew my life would never measure up. It couldn't. But, he came to me anyway. Like Peter, I was given grace, and because of his grace, I am compelled to follow.

There is an awesome scene in the Bible that illustrates the grace of Jesus and the love he has for us, despite our shortcomings. As Jesus foreknew, Peter's final act toward him prior to his death was betrayal. As Jesus was getting brutally beaten and murdered, Peter refused to help. Worse, he pretended that he did not know him.

After the crucifixion of Jesus, when Mary went to the tomb early Sunday morning, the stone has been rolled away and there was an angel greeting her. Mary must have been startled beyond belief. She looked on in amazement. Jesus had risen! Everything he said was true!

Mark 16:7 captures the heart of Jesus. The angel turned to Mary and said, "Go, tell his disciples *and Peter*" (author's emphasis). Go and tell Peter. The one who had denied him and refused to acknowledge him. The one who was certainly hurting more than anyone else because he had turned his back on Jesus. The angel said to make sure Peter knew that Jesus had risen. Jesus cared for Peter and wanted him to know that everything was okay. "Forget about the sins, Peter. Just know that I have risen."

After receiving the news, Peter recklessly told others. As Jesus said in Luke 7:47, Peter had been forgiven much, so he loved Jesus much.

Again, the same is true in my life. As you read my story, you see that I have been forgiven much. Thank God for a Christ who overlooks it all and clears my guilt. He who has been forgiven much loves Jesus much. This, my friends, is the definition of grace. May it be true in your life as well.

The anchor holds.

My Personal Reflection on my Journey

9 Lessons (from The Anchor)

My journey has involved adventure, risk, folly, and forgiveness. More than anything, I want my kids to capture what I learned only later in life. I want them to recognize the value of knowing and following a holy God early in their walks so they don't have to experience the folly of youth, as Solomon says. With that, I will share some lessons that I want my kids to recognize early on, which I believe others can benefit from as well.

Lesson 1: Read and know the Bible.

Every bit of advice that I now give anyone begins with Scripture. The Bible is the lens through which I view the world. This lens will never lead you astray. The world, our culture, will constantly push against the words in the Bible, challenge those words. But, the words of God stand the test of time. The words of God are true. A life lived with this lens is a life of joy.

Lesson 2: Love the Jesus of the Bible.

The Bible is a book about your Savior. Many in the Bible knew the Scriptures without knowing the Savior. Develop a personal passion for Jesus that will fuel your life, your love for others. All other fires will be extinguished. This fire will remain forever.

Lesson 3: Understand the personal threads woven into your fabric.

As you have seen in my life, you are made up of threads from your heritage and history. Embrace these threads. This is how God made you, the life he gave you. Do not only embrace them, though. Know the threads intimately, because each one has positive and negative attributes. Know them enough to accentuate the positive and beware the negative. God gave you the negative as a warning.

Lesson 4: Cherish relationships, family and friends.

God gave us relationships as a gift. Recognize this. Don't take relationships for granted. When the going gets tough, you need people in your life who love you. Write a note to someone close to you today.

Lesson 5: Don't make mountains out of molehills.

Don't let the small issues of life become big issues. Let the molehills remain molehills. There are going to be some major issues in your journey. Times will come that rock your world. Storms will come that challenge your faith. As Adrian Rogers used to say, "You are either headed to a storm, in a storm, or coming out of a storm." Take the small issues in stride so that you have energy for the big ones.

Lesson 6: Control money; don't let it control you.

Jesus warned of money. He knew the danger that loomed with materiality. Recognize money as a gift and manage it wisely. Always be a giver, not one who goes after things.

Lesson 7: Don't judge others.

In our culture today, the focus of many a conversation is other people. We eat people for lunch. God, however, is the only judge. Learn from my life that everyone messes up. We are not the ones to point fingers, call people out. We are ones who love, no matter what.

Lesson 8: Fear is a trigger for action, a sign to move forward, to follow God and push through.

Never let fear stop you from doing. In fact, if you fear something, go after it hard. When you do, doors will open and you will see the world differently. God will lead you to places you never imagined. When you feel fear, recognize it and follow it.

Lesson 9: Don't follow culture; follow God.

God has a unique plan for your life. Culture will tell you otherwise, but don't copy it. Lean on Romans 12:2 to discover his will for your life. Then, recklessly go after it. You go after it, and let him provide the safety. Culture calls. So does Jesus.

Follow him.

Nine lessons. Nail them on your door post. Live them and you will live well.

Lessons from your Journey

NOTE: These lessons could quite possibly be the greatest treasure you leave your kids, future generations. My kids each have these framed in their bedrooms.

A Parting Word about The Seasons Journal

If you completed the journal, congratulations. You have just created a treasure for your family and future generations, one that few people have as a record for their loved ones. I hope you learned a little more about yourself along the way.

My encouragement to you is to pass this on to others. I believe that we each can positively influence others by giving the gift of our story. We each have a story to tell.

Psalm 107:2 – Has the Lord redeemed you? Then speak out!

I would love to hear your thoughts or comments at impactothers.blog.

A Parting Word about The Anchor

The quality of anything in my life is directly proportional to my biblical literacy.

I like to read. Look in my briefcase at any given time and you will find a couple of nonfiction business books. I don't read just anything, though. I feel that if I am going to invest time in reading, I need to get something out of it. That's just me.

Without exception, I believe the most underutilized, underappreciated book is the Bible. Whether you are a Christian, an atheist, a believer in God, whatever, the Bible is an invaluable resource for history, a view of mankind. It is a literary masterpiece. As an avid reader of the Bible, I have learned how the practical advice of this book will lead one to a successful, rich life.

A great example is the book of Ecclesiastes in the Bible, an autobiography written by King Solomon. Who would not cherish the insight of the wealthiest man on earth during his time, the King of Israel, an architect, an entrepreneur, a man with unsurpassed wisdom? Recounting his days, he describes his business accomplishments, his wealth, as nothing but "vanity" (Ecc. 1:2 ESV). Solomon found what we describe as success in the world to be nothing but vanity once acquired. In our day, how many times have you heard those who seemingly have it all describe life as empty? We run, we search, we acquire, only to find that everything is vanity. Solomon told us this truth before we ever started the race.

No doubt, Ecclesiastes is a rich book of insight that our society leaves to gather dust. And, the Bible is full of sixty-six books like Ecclesiastes.

Unfortunately, our culture has turned the Bible into a book that divides, that is full of friction. My challenge to people is to pick the book up and see what it says for yourself. The book is an underutilized gift that I discovered later in life. No matter your stage of life, wisdom of the Bible awaits.

www.ingramcontent.com/pod-product-compliance
Lightning Source LLC
Chambersburg PA
CBHW011141290426
44108CB00023B/2711